This book belongs to

. . . .

Acknowledgments

Thanks to the following for generously supporting the publication of this book:

Rodney Bisiker	Tim Evans	Simon Lloyd
James Butler	Steve and Kate Forss	Mike Mogridge
John Bowler	Ed Gadd	Ivor Whittle

Legasee is enormously grateful to the mums, dads and children within Help For Heroes' Band of Sisters who have shared their stories of adversity and inspiration in the hope that these will help other families in similar situations.

Thanks also to all the people who play The National Lottery.

HERITAGE FUND

First printed in 2020

A CIP Catalogue record for this book is available from the British Library.
ISBN number 978-1-83853-780-7

Design by Jordan Atkinson
Printed by Hill Print Limited

Say Hello to some new friends

Sam and her Dad
Page 06

Ruby and
her Mum
Page 16

Ollie and
his Dad
Page 24

Sam's Dad

Sam thinks her dad is the best daddy ever,

He's funny and silly and cuddly and clever.

His job's in the Navy, he works with machines

Deep under the sea in the big submarines.

And sometimes he works far away for a while,

Sam misses his hugs and she misses his smile,

But when he comes back everything seems alright

'Cause Sam has her daddy to cuddle up tight.

Then after last summer Sam's dad was deployed,

And when he came back he was always annoyed,

He didn't like going for walks with their puppy,

He wouldn't throw balls or play keepy-uppy.

And lately when Sam plays a match with her team

Her dad looks quite lost like he's in a daydream,

And whilst her mum claps, it just isn't the same

Not having them both cheer her on in the game!

Sam's dad used to love it on bonfire night

With sparklers and fireworks, but not so tonight!

As soon as the first of the rockets shot out,

He dropped to the floor and he started to shout.

Sam was embarrassed but also quite scared,

And everyone out there just pointed and stared,

So mummy decided it's best to go home

Where daddy can have quiet time on his own.

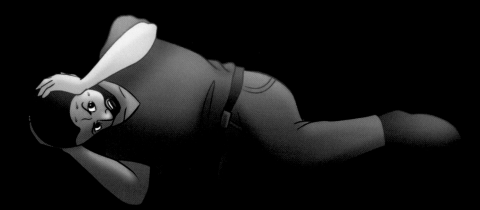

In her pyjamas and tucked up in bed

Sam's mummy sat down and she kissed her forehead.

"I know that was scary, but dad is okay,

"It's just sometimes he has a really bad day."

She said, "You remember when you cut your knee

"On that rusty nail sticking out of a tree?

"And how the nurse had to give you an injection

"To help make you better and stop an infection."

Then at your next checkup, you thought that you'd get
Another injection so you got upset.
"But I didn't," said Sam "He just looked at it,
"And it didn't hurt me, not one little bit!"

"Yes!" Said Sam's mum "but you thought that it might

"And that's like what happened to your dad tonight."

"'When sometimes we think that what happened before

"Will happen again 'cause of something we saw…"

"…or something we heard, or something we felt,

"Or sometimes it's possibly something we smelt.

"The fireworks went bang and reminded your dad

"Of a different noise that made him feel sad."

"And even though daddy feels safe now he's back

"He remembers a time when it wasn't like that,

"So he stays on the lookout so he's always ready

"To take the best care of you, me and teddy."

"And when dad gets cross he's not angry at us,

"So we don't have to worry or make a big fuss.

"Until he feels calm we can leave him alone

"And find lots of nice things to do on our own."

Sam asked, "How can we make sure dad feels okay?

"So he doesn't feel bad like he felt today?"

And mummy said "you should just keep being you,

"Your daddy loves all of the things that you do."

Then daddy came upstairs to hug Sam goodnight,

And Sam knew that everything would be alright.

Her dad is still funny and cuddly and clever

And they can take care of each other forever.

Ruby's Mum

Daddy says he knows for sure where Ruby gets her brains,

Her mummy's in the RAF, she mends the broken planes,

And sometimes with her job she travels very far away,

But when she comes back home, she and Ruby love to play.

When Ruby goes in goal, mummy tries to kick it past,

And when they go out on their bikes, mum cycles really fast.

On nature walks they like to look for different leaves and flowers,

And in the playground mummy pushes Ruby's swing for hours.

But then one rainy Friday, Ruby's mummy had to go

To work in a place far away that Ruby didn't know.

So daddy made a calendar so they could count and track

Each month and week and day there was until her mum came back.

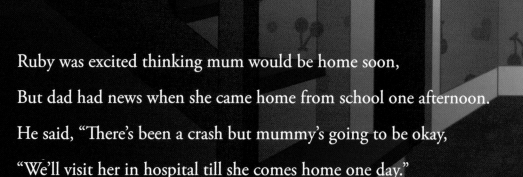

Ruby was excited thinking mum would be home soon,

But dad had news when she came home from school one afternoon.

He said, "There's been a crash but mummy's going to be okay,

"We'll visit her in hospital till she comes home one day."

The day arrived and Ruby stood excited in the hall,

Dad pushed mummy's wheelchair in the door and scraped the wall,

And that's when Ruby ran up to her room to have a cry

Why wasn't mummy standing up? She wouldn't even try!

Ruby wondered how her mum would do the normal things,

Like kicking balls or riding bikes or pushing her on swings.

She worried that they'd never do a nature walk together

'Cause it would be too hard to push a wheelchair round forever.

Then Ruby came downstairs and told her mum why she was scared,

And then they had the biggest hug the two had ever shared.

Then mummy said, "You know that I've been really worried too,

"But with our heads together we'll find great new things to do!"

So they did lots of different stuff whilst mum was getting fitter,

Like baking cakes and making cards from paper, glue and glitter.

Soon mummy was an expert in her wheelchair she could boast,

And so they both set out to do the things they liked the most.

They went down to the park where Ruby climbed onto the swing,

And mummy pushed her up so high she could see everything,

And when they used the roundabout mum hung on to the side,

Which pulled her wheelchair round so fast they laughed until they cried!

Their favourite nature walk became a nature 'roll' you see.

Ruby picked the plants and mummy kept them on her knee.

And football's changed as mum can't be a striker any more -

She went in goal instead, whilst daddy helped to keep the score.

And going out on bikes mum has three wheels instead of two,

Her hands move special pedals like the Paralympians do.

Going out together gives them all a real thrill,

And no-one can catch mummy when she rides her bike downhill!

So Ruby's mummy told her that whilst things do sometimes change,

She shouldn't be too worried if she feels scared or strange,

The most important thing is that they all have lots of fun,

''Now, I'll set off downhill and let's see how fast you can run!''

Ollie's Dad

Ollie's dad's a soldier and he thinks that's pretty cool,

It means his life is different to most other kids at school,

'Cause when your dad's a soldier moving isn't all that strange,

But Ollie still gets worried when he knows that things will change.

And change makes Ollie nervous - it turns his knees to jelly,

And then those worries flip and flop around in Ollie's belly.

It's like a hundred bunnies ate a hundred jumping beans,

Then jumped and bounced and jiggled on a hundred trampolines!

So this year when his parents told him they would move again

Away from all his school friends and the park on Churchill Lane,

The bunnies all came back again to hop and skip and jump

Until his hands felt sweaty and his heart was going thump!

"I know it can feel scary to move far away," said mummy

"And sometimes even mums and dads get bunnies in their tummy.

"But even though your friends at school don't move house like we do,

"I bet there's lots of things that get their bunnies jumping too."

And that made Ollie think about the new girl in his year,

She was good at sport and spelling and her name was Sophie-Mia.

He remembered Sophie-Mia said her mum was in the Navy,

And how she'd moved at least three times since she was just a baby.

Ollie's face lit up – he'd had a brilliant idea!

He'd see if he could get advice and help from Sophie-Mia.

So when he asked his new friend for the best thing he could do,

She told him that when she moved schools she found it scary too.

She said "do you remember how I cried on my first day?

"I had nobody to talk to and I didn't want to play.

"But Mrs. Fisher sat me next to William and Grace,

"They stopped me feeling sad and put a smile back on my face".

"And soon I'd made a lot of friends and really settled down,

"And mummy lets me talk to all my friends from my old town."

"Two lots of friends?" Said Ollie "Wow! That would be really cool!

And maybe it's exciting to start in a different school."

"I'm sure I'll meet a lot of kids who I'll like even more,

"Plus I'll have a new bedroom and new places to explore.

"Thank you Sophie-Mia, I hope we can stay in touch."

Sophie Mia smiled and said "I'd like that very much."

So Ollie told his mum and dad that moving's not so bad,

And now he's quite excited, and really rather glad.

Some things will stay the same for him, he'll still have dad and mummy,

One more thing would make it perfect… ''can we get a bunny?!''

When Legasee Educational Trust first started working with Help for Heroes, we never thought we'd end up writing children's stories...

Legasee
The Veterans Video Archive

BAND *of* SISTERS
Support for the Families

Legasee provides students, teachers and military researchers with unique access to filmed interviews with military personnel who have served their country at some point between 1939 and the present day, and is now the UK's largest, freely available online film archive of this aspect of the UK's military history.

From the Normandy beaches to the mountains of Korea, airlifting supplies in Berlin and playing concerts to locals in the Middle East, we have heard many veterans talk about the impact that their military service has had on their families.

And that is how we met the Band of Sisters....

The Help for Heroes' Band of Sisters is a membership network open to the close supporting family members of veterans, service personnel and those who have served alongside our armed forces who have been wounded, injured or sick during, or as a result of, their service and resulting in an ongoing need for support.

Offering advice and support both practical and emotional they care for the carers, organising get-togethers as well as respite weekends at their unique facilities. Phoenix House at Catterick Garrison offers families a place to relax, have fun and just be, with a sisterhood where shared experiences and genuine understanding make a huge difference to military families.

So, about these stories?

As we began to gather first-hand accounts detailing the struggles of parents, partners and children who are living with someone affected by a physical or mental injury, we were told of a real lack of stories to support children to understand their own situation. Parents, schools and libraries needed literature to help children to better comprehend their changing world, including those for whom moving home as part of military life causes significant upheaval.

Peer reviewed by parents and children in military families, we are delighted to have been able to produce this meaningful resource and hope that it has helped your family today.

Written by Paula Rogers and illustrated by Geraldina Sierra the stories were produced in conjunction with Le Cateau Primary School and the Catterick, Richmond and Colburn Community Libraries group. The project is generously supported by the National Lottery Heritage Fund and the Armed Forces Covenant Fund Trust.

www.legasee.org.uk

Can you Help?

This book is just one of the creative ways that we use the personal stories of our armed forces veterans.

Legasee was created from a desire to develop national pride, personal resilience and selflessness in the generations to come, by ensuring the legacy of our countrymen's amazing contribution to freedom and peace is never forgotten.

If you believe that what we are doing is important, please help us by sending a gift. Any amount, however small is sincerely appreciated.

I would like to help Legasee record more interviews with veterans.

As a single donation (enclosed) of: £.....................

A regular monthly gift of: £.....................

Name ....

Address ....

....

....

Postcode ....

Tel ....

Email ....

Signed ....

Date ....

☐ I am a UK taxpayer and DECLARE that I want Legasee Educational Trust to treat all donations I make from the date of this declaration until I notify you otherwise as Gift Aid donations.